28 Popular No-Kne

Updated to Include New

from the kitchen of
Artisan Bread with Steve

By
Steve Gamelin

Bread Theory:

Bakers have known for years that
bread benefits from long proofing times.
The traditional no-knead method takes advantage of this principle.
It uses a minimum amount of yeast
and long proofing time to develop flavor.
Meanwhile, the long proofing time
replaces the arduous task of kneading...
Mother Nature does the work for you.

Table of Contents

"Table of Contents" lists both recipes and bakeware used to shape loaves and rolls, but you can mix and match… the ingredients from one recipe with the bakeware (method) from a different recipe. The two components are independent of each other. For example, you can use the ingredients from the "Cheddar Cheese Bread (Dutch oven)" recipe… proof for 8 to 24 hours… then use the bakeware from the "Classic White Bread (standard bread pan)" recipe. In other words… you can bake cheddar cheese bread in the standard bread pan by following the classic white recipe's standard bread pan method. Any recipe… any bakeware.

Letter from Steve

The no-knead bread method has revolutionized bread baking. The average family can now have fresh from the oven bakery quality artisan bread in the convenience of their own home with little or no-kneading... Mother Nature does the kneading for you. No-yeast proofing... instant yeast does not need to be proofed in warm water prior to using. No mixer... ingredients can be combined with a spoon. It's almost as easy as making a bowl of *Campbell's* soup.

This is "New Age Bread Baking". I understand what Italian bread, French bread, and baguettes are, and I understand the proper techniques for making those breads, but we live in a new age and we should embrace new ideas. Instead of trying to emulate the bread methods of the past we should focus on our goal... to make great tasting, bakery quality, artisan bread with the methods and techniques that fit our busy schedules.

My Philosophy

I believe in "Smart & Easy". Note, I didn't say fast and cheap. I make no-knead bread because it's the smartest, easiest, way to make bakery quality artisan bread and I believe my readers and subscribers are attracted to the no-knead method for the same reasons. In response to my readers and subscribers, I strive for convenience and address each recipe from a very practical standpoint... as, I believe, they would want me to develop my recipes.

Smart: In the design of each recipe I try to be smart. I do my best to pick ingredients that are practical, reasonably priced, and easily available. I stay away from complex overlapping flavors and I use ingredients in moderation. More is not always better.

Easy: I look at each step in my recipes and try to simplify it. One of my most successful innovations was using an 8" skillet as a proofing basket. It shapes the dough during proofing and the handle makes it so easy to carry the dough to the baking vessel that even your kids could do it safely.

And I don't have a baker, food stylist or professional photographer... I baked the breads and took the pictures. My pictures are not as good as a professional photographer, but they accurately portray the results you can expect.

My Specialty

My specialty is to take the world's simplest list of ingredients (flour, salt, yeast and water) using the world's easiest bread making method (no mixer, no kneading, no yeast proofing) to create artisan breads that you would be proud to serve your family, friends and guests. One recipe, one method... with minor modifications I can make anything from a boule to an old-fashioned cinnamon roll.

I think you'll enjoy this cookbook.

Steve

"I know when food is supposed to be served in a bowl with a name on it."
Fran Fine - "The Nanny"

When you look at a recipe,
think of it as sheet music.
It's the instrument and voice that transforms
sheet music into a song and gives it individuality.

Recipes are written for general use
waiting for the right instrument (bakeware) and voice (baker)
to transform the recipe
into a unique artisan loaf.

I hope you enjoy this cookbook.

Steve

The Two Basic Methods for Making No-Knead Bread

There are two basic methods... traditional and turbo.

"Traditional" No-Knead Method
The traditional no knead method uses long proofing times (8 to 12 hours) to develop flavor and was designed to be baked in a Dutch oven. The purpose of the Dutch oven is to emulate a baker's oven by trapping the moisture from the dough in a "screaming" hot, enclosed environment. This is an excellent method for making artisan quality bread.

Recommended YouTube video: <u>World's Easiest No-Knead Bread (Introducing "Hands-Free" Technique)</u>

No-Knead "Turbo" Method
The no-knead "Turbo Method" uses shorter proofing times (ready to bake in 2-1/2 hours) and was designed to be baked in traditional bakeware (bread pan, etc.). It was designed for those who want to make no-knead bread, but... don't want to wait 8 to 24 hours. Those who want bread machine bread, but... don't want to buy and store a bread machine. It's for those of you who want a fast reliable way to make fresh from the oven bread without the hustle of expensive machines, Dutch ovens, or kneading.

Recommended YouTube video: <u>Ultimate Introduction to No-Knead "Turbo" Bread... ready to bake in 2-1/2 hours</u>

This cookbook uses the "traditional" method of making no-knead bread.

Ingredients

It only takes four ingredients to make bread... flour, salt, yeast and water.

Flour

Flour is the base ingredient of bread and there are four basic types of flour...

(1) <u>Bread flour</u> is designed for yeast bread. It has a higher percentage of gluten which gives artisan bread its airy crumb.

(2) <u>All-purpose flour</u> has less gluten than bread flour. I use all-purpose flour for biscuits, flatbreads, etc. In other words... I use it when I don't want an airy crumb.

(3) <u>Self-rising flour</u> is all-purpose flour with baking soda and baking powder added as leavening agents. It's intended for quick breads... premixed and ready to go. Do not use self-rising flour to make yeast bread. To see the difference between yeast and quick breads you may want to watch <u>Introduction to No-Knead Beer Bread (a.k.a. Artisan Yeast Beer Bread)</u> and <u>Introduction to Quick Beer Bread (a.k.a. Beer Bread Dinner Rolls)</u>.

(4) And there are a variety of <u>specialty flours</u>... whole wheat, rye, and a host of others. Each has its unique flavor and characteristics. In some cases, you can substitute specialty flour for bread flour, but you may need to tweak the recipe because most specialty flours have less gluten. I frequently blend specialty flour with bread flour.

Flour is the primary ingredient... if you don't use the correct flour you won't get the desired results.

Note: To know how many cups of flour there are in a specific bag... it's typically on the side in "Nutritional Facts". For example, this bag reads, "Serving Size 1/4 cup... Serving Per Container about 75". In other words... 18.75 (75 times 1/4). That's the technical answer, but in the real world (measuring cup versus weight) a bag of flour will measure differently based on density (sifted versus unsifted), type of flour (wheat is more dense than bread flour), humidity (flour weighs more on humid days), and all the other variables life and nature have to offer. There is no single correct answer, but for practical purposes... figure a 5# bag of bread flour is 17 to 18 cups.

Salt

While it is possible to make bread without salt... you would be disappointed. There are three basics types of salt...

(1) Most baking recipes are designed to use everyday <u>table salt</u> unless specified otherwise. Unless you're experienced, it is probably smartest to use table salt for your baking needs.

(2) <u>Kosher salt</u> is excellent. I use it when I cook, but a tablespoon of kosher salt does not equal a tablespoon of table salt because kosher salt crystals are larger.

(3) And, I use <u>specialty salt</u> as a garnish... for appearance and taste. For example, I use sea salt to garnish pretzels.

Generally speaking, when salt is added as an ingredient and baked it is difficult to taste the difference between table, kosher and sea salt. When salt is added as a garnish and comes in contact with the taste buds... kosher or specialty salt is an excellent choice.

Yeast

Yeast is the "magic" ingredient which transforms flour and water into dough. My traditional no-knead recipes use 1/4 tsp yeast... I want the dough to rise slowly which allows the dough to develop flavor. My "Turbo" recipes use 1-1/4 tsp yeast... I want a faster rises like traditional bread recipes. There are three basic types of yeast...

(1) The most common is <u>active dry yeast</u> which needs to be proof in warm water prior to being added to flour.

(2) I use <u>instant dry yeast</u> (a.k.a. "instant yeast", "bread machine yeast", "quick rise", "rapid rise", "fast rising", etc.) which does not need to be proofed in warm water. It is a more recent development which is more potent and reliable... and why worry about proofing yeast if you don't have too.

(3) Some older recipes call for <u>cake yeast</u> (a.k.a. "compressed yeast" or "fresh yeast"), but it's perishable. Most bakers substitute active dry and instant yeast for cake yeast when using older recipes.

The names on the bottles can be confusing. When in doubt, read the instructions and look for one that does not require soaking the yeast in warm water prior to use.

Water

Water hydrates the ingredients and activates the yeast. The no-knead method uses a little more water than the typical recipe... and that's a good thing. It makes it easier to combine the wet and dry ingredients, and contributes to its airy crumb.

(1) I use <u>cool tap water</u>. It's convenient and easy, but sometimes city water has too much chlorine (chlorine kills yeast).

(2) If your dough does not rise during first proofing you may want to use <u>bottled drinking water</u>.

(3) But, do not use <u>distilled water</u> because the minerals have been removed.

Water is a flavor ingredient, if your water doesn't taste good... use bottled drinking water.

Other Ingredients
Some recipes will include sugar, eggs, milk, vegetable oil, shortening, and a variety of other ingredients... each has its purpose, but I prefer the basics (flour, salt, yeast and water) because it gives me bakery quality artisan bread with a beautiful airy crumb... you'll love the flavor.

Flavor Ingredients
It only takes four ingredients to make bread... flour, salt, yeast and water, to which a variety of flavor ingredients can be added to make specialty breads such as... honey whole wheat, multi-grain white, rosemary, Mediterranean olive, cinnamon raisin, honey oatmeal, and a host of others.

Technique & Tips

The technique discussed in this section is demonstrated on YouTube in <u>World's Easiest No-Knead Bread (Introducing "Hands-Free" Technique)</u>.

Combining Ingredients

Start with the liquid ingredients. Pour cool tap water to a 3 to 4 qt glass mixing bowl. Then add salt and yeast... and stir to combine (it will insure the salt and yeast are evenly distributed throughout the water). Then add the flour (flour will resist the water and float). Start by stirring the ingredients with the handle end of a plastic spoon drawing the flour from the sides into the middle of bowl (vigorously mixing will not hydrate the flour faster... but it will raise a lot of dust). Within 30 seconds the flour will hydrate and form a shaggy ball. Then change direction of the stirring and tumble the dough to combine the moist flour on the bottom with the dry flour on top (about 10 seconds). Finish by scraping flour from the side of the bowl and incorporating. It takes about one minute to combine the wet and dry ingredients.

Cover bowl with plastic wrap and place in a warm draft free location to proof for 8 to 24 hours.

1st Proofing (Bulk Fermentation)

The process is called "proofing" because it "proves" your yeast is active. If your bread doesn't rise the usual culprits are... outdated yeast or chlorinated water (chlorine kills yeast). Solution, get fresh yeast and/or use bottled drinking water.

Bread making is nature at work (yeast is a living organism) and subject to nature. Seasons (summer vs. winter) and weather (heat & humidity) have a direct impact on proofing. In other words, don't worry if your dough varies in size... that's Mother Nature at work. Just focus on your goal... if the gluten forms (the dough has a stringy nature) and doubles in size... you're good to go.

Tip: Bread can be proofed in a wide range of temperatures and conditions (our ancestor didn't have heating or air conditioning... they proofed their dough in a wide range of temperatures and conditions for centuries), but it is important to proof your dough in a warm draft free setting (the ideal temperature for yeast is 78 to 85 degrees F). If you don't have a warm draft-free setting to proof your dough (and it hasn't doubled in size)... extend the proofing time. For example, on cold winter days with no sunlight... I proof over night.

Degas, Pull & Stretch

The purpose of degassing, pulling and stretching is to, (a) expel the gases that formed during bulk fermentation, (b) strengthen the dough by realigning and stretching the gluten strands, and (c) stimulate yeast activity for 2nd proofing.

Because no-knead dough is sticky and difficult to handle... I degas, pull & stretch dough by stirring it with the handle end of a plastic spoon in the bowl (like a dough hook). It will reduce the size of the dough ball by 50% making it easier to handle and the process replaces folding and shaping in most cases.

Roll to Coat

Before removing the dough from bowl... dust the dough and side of the bowl with flour, then roll to coat. The flour will bond to the sticky dough making it easier to handle, but do not roll to coat with flour if you're going to "Garnish & Baste".

Garnish & Baste (optional)

The purpose of garnishing and basting is to enhance the appearance of the crust, but it isn't necessary. If you decide to garnish and baste there are two techniques... roll to coat and skillet method.

Roll to Coat Method: Before removing dough from bowl... add ingredients to bowl (on the dough and side of the bowl), then roll to coat. For example, when I garnish honey oatmeal bread... I sprinkle oat in the bowl and on the dough, then roll the dough ball in the oats and they will bond to the sticky dough. This can also be done with seeds, grains, olive oil, egg wash, etc.

Skillet Method: When I want to garnish and/or baste the top of the loaf... I coat the proofing skillet with baste (egg wash, olive oil, vegetable oil, etc.) and sprinkle with the garnish (oats, seeds, grains, etc.). The ingredients will bond with the dough as the dough proofs.

Supporting video: How to Garnish & Baste No-Knead Bread using "Hands-Free" Technique

Divide & Shape

If you're not going to divide the dough... it can go straight from the mixing bowl to the proofing or baking vessel. If you are going to divide and shape the dough... roll the dough ball out of the bowl (excess flour and all) onto the work surface to divide and shape. Then add flour to the work surface as needed... it will make it easier. I use a plastic bowl scraper to assist in dividing, shaping and carrying the dough to the baking vessel. Together they (flour & bowl scraper) make it easier to handle the dough.

2nd Proofing

Second proofing is more temperature sensitive because of its shorter proofing time (1 to 2 hours). I generally proof for 1-1/2 hours on warm days and 2 hours on colder days.

Score (optional)

The purpose of scoring dough is to provide seams to control where the crust will split during "oven spring", but it isn't necessary to score dough. If you do decide to score your loaf you may want to use a scissors (no-knead dough is very moist and more likely to stretch than slice). Personally, I place the dough in the baking vessel seam side up... the dough will split at the seam during "oven spring" which gives the loaf a nice rustic appearance.

Bake

Baking Time: Bread is done when it reaches an internal temperature of 185 to 220 degrees F and the crumb (inside of the bread) isn't doughy. Baking times in my recipes are designed to give bread an internal temperature of 200 to 205 degrees F, but ovens vary and you may need to adjust your baking times slightly.

No-Stick Spray: Most bakeware has a non-stick surface, but it is safest to spray your bakeware unless you are fully confident your bread won't stick.

Ovens: Ovens don't always tell the truth. I check the temperature of ovens and bakeware. Ovens with a digital readout that displays the temperature as they preheat are typically very accurate, but ovens that say they will be at temperature in a specific number of minutes are not always accurate. My point is... you will get the best results if you learn the character and nature of your oven.

Oven Rack: Generally speaking you want to bake bread and rolls in the middle or lower third of the oven, but it isn't critical. Just keep them away from the upper heating element or they may brown a little too quickly.

Oven Spring: When dough is first put into the oven they will increase in size by as much as a third in a matter of minutes because, (a) gases trapped in the dough will expand, (b) moisture will turn into steam and try to push its way out, and (c) yeast will become highly active converting sugars into gases. The steam and gases work together to create "oven spring". Once the internal temperature of the bread reaches 120 degrees F... the yeast will begin to die and the crust will harden.

Equipment & Bakeware

Bowl for Mixing: You can use any 3 to 4 qt bowl. I use a 3-1/2 qt glass bowl because, (a) there's ample room for the dough to expand, (b) plastic wrap sticks to glass, and (c) I don't want the rim of my bowl to exceed the width of the plastic wrap.

Measuring Cups and Spoons for Dry Ingredients: I'm sure you already have measuring cups and spoons in the house... they will work just fine. If you're going to buy new, I prefer oval versus round because an oval shape will fit into jars and containers more easily.

Measuring Cups for Liquid Ingredients: The only difference between dry and liquid measuring cups is the spout... they're identical in volume, but dry measuring cups are intended to measure volume while liquid measuring cups are intended to measure mass (neither measures weight). Thus, recipes are generally designed to use measuring cups and spoons, versus a scale.

Note: U.S. and metric measuring cups may be used interchangeably... there is only a slight difference (±3%). More importantly, the ingredients of a recipe measured with a set (U.S. or metric) will have their volumes in the same proportion to one another.

Spoon for Combining Wet and Dry Ingredients: A spoon is an excellent tool for combining wet and dry ingredients. Surprisingly, I found the handle end of a plastic spoon worked best for me because, I didn't have a big clump on the end like I did with some of my other mixing utensils (which makes it a lot easier to stir and manipulate the dough). And when you think about it... mixers don't use a paddle to mix dough, they use a hook which looks a lot like the handle end of my spoon.

Silicon Mat: Silicone mats are very useful... I use them as reusable parchment paper (they're environmentally friendly). Silicone mats serve two purposes... (a) as a work surface for folding and shaping (they have excellent non-stick properties), and (b) as a baking mat... specifically when the dough is difficult to move after folding and shaping. And I slide a cookie sheet under the silicone mat before baking (it makes it easier to put the mat into and take them out of the oven).

Spatula: I use a spatula to scrape the sides of the bowl to get the last bits of flour incorporated into the dough.

Plastic Bowl Scraper: I use a plastic bowl scraper verses a dough scraper because it's the better multi-tasker. I use the bowl scraper to (a) fold, shape, and divide the dough, (b) assist in carrying the dough it to the proofing vessel, (c) then I use it to scrape the excess flour off the work surface, (d) scrape the excess flour out of the bowl (after all it is a bowl scraper), and (e) scrape any remaining bits in the sink towards the disposal. It's a useful multi-tasker.

Timer: I'm sure you already have a timer in the house. Any that you already have will work just fine. I prefer digital because they're more accurate.

Proofing Baskets & Vessels: The purpose of a proofing basket or vessel is to pre-shape the dough prior to baking (dough will spread if it isn't contained). Because no-knead dough has a tendency to stick to the lining of proofing baskets... I use common household items as proofing vessels. For example, I use an 8" skillet (with no-stick spray) to pre-shape dough when baking in a Dutch oven. It shapes the dough during proofing, and the handle makes it easy to carry the dough and put it in the hot Dutch oven safely.

You can also proof dough in the baking vessel if it doesn't have to be preheated. For example, standard loaves are typically proof and baked in the bread pan where your bread pan shapes the loaf during proofing and baking. You can use this same principle for shaping and baking rolls and buns.

Baking Vessels: Baking vessels come in a variety of sizes, shapes and materials. You can change the appearance of the loaf by sampling changing the baking vessel.

Proofing Towel: Any lint-free towel can be used to cover your dough during 2nd proofing.

Cooling Rack: The purpose of a cooling rack is to expose the bottom of the loaf during the cooling process.

Bread Bags: I use plastic bread bags to keep our bread after they have cooled. And, when I give bread as gifts... I use plastic bags for bread that have cooled and paper bags when the bread is still warm (I don't want to trap the moisture in a plastic bag).

Breads

One simple recipe... four ingredients, no mixer, no kneading, no yeast proofing... just a little tweaking and you can create a variety of artisan breads that you would be proud to serve your family, friends and guests.

I will be using a variety of different baking vessels/methods to make the breads... Dutch oven, long baker, baking stone, baguette pan, parchment paper, silicone pad, and a rimmed baking sheet... and, generally speaking you can take the ingredients from one recipe and use the baking vessel/method from a different recipe. Thus, if you wish to bake the caraway rye bread in a Dutch oven... take the ingredients from the caraway rye bread recipe and use the method and baking times from a recipe using a Dutch oven... baking for 30 minutes with the top on and 3 to 15 minutes with the top off.

Country White Bread (Dutch oven)

Country White is the most popular artisan bread. It's simple… it's basic… and it will give you a gorgeous loaf. I use a 2.6 qt *Emile Henry* flame top ceramic Dutch oven to shape this loaf.

Notes: If I want everyday bread with a chewy crust—similar to *La Brea's* Country White—I bake it for 3 to 5 minutes with the top off. If I want a rustic loaf with a dark harder crust I bake it for 10 to 15 minutes with the top off.

Country White Bread

Pour water into a 3 to 4 qt glass mixing bowl.

> 12 oz cool tap Water

Add salt and yeast... give a quick stir to combine.

> 1-1/2 tsp Salt
>
> 1/4 tsp Instant Yeast

Add flour... stir until dough forms a shaggy ball, then tumble dough to combine moist flour on the bottom with dry flour, scrape flour from side of bowl and finish combining.

> 3 cups Bread Flour

Cover bowl with plastic wrap, place in a warm draft-free location, and proof for 8 to 24 hours.

8 to 24 hours later (Dutch oven)

When dough has risen and developed its gluten structure... spray an 8" proofing skillet with no-stick cooking spray and set aside.

Start by putting handle end of spoon in center of dough and "degas, pull and stretch" dough to form a ball.

Generously dust dough and side of bowl with flour... roll dough in flour to coat. Roll dough out of bowl into proofing skillet.

Place proofing skillet in a warm draft-free location, cover with a lint-free towel, and proof for 1 to 2 hours.

1 to 2 hours later

Before dough is fully proofed... move rack to lower third of oven, place baking vessel in oven, and pre-heat to 450 degrees F.

When oven has come to temperature...

Remove baking vessel from oven, transfer dough from proofing skillet to baking vessel, score (optional) and bake for 30 minutes with the top on and 3 to 15 minutes with the top off depending on how rustic (hard) you like your crust.

30 to 45 minutes later

Gently turn loaf out on work surface and place on cooling rack.

Boulis Gigiantious (large Dutch oven)

There are times when it would be nice to have a larger loaf and there isn't a law that says you can't make large loaves using the no-knead method. This recipe gives you a 50% larger boule which makes full use of a large Dutch oven. I used a 4 qt *Giada de Laurentiis* cast iron braiser pan with lid to make the larger loaf.

Notes: This is the standard no-knead Country White recipe increased by 50%. The dough will fit in the 3-1/2 qt glass mixing bowl, but you will need to use a 10" non-stick skillet for 2nd proofing and the baking time was increased 10 minutes to account for its larger size.

Boulis Gigiantious

Pour water into a 3-1/2 to 4 qt glass mixing bowl.

18 oz cool tap Water

Add salt and yeast... give a quick stir to combine.

2-1/4 tsp Salt

1/2 tsp Instant Yeast

Add flour... stir until dough forms a shaggy ball, then tumble dough to combine moist flour on the bottom with dry flour, scrape flour from side of bowl and finish combining.

4-1/2 cups Bread Flour

Cover bowl with plastic wrap, place in a warm draft-free location, and proof for 8 to 24 hours.

8 to 24 hours later (large Dutch oven)

When dough has risen and developed its gluten structure... spray a 10" proofing skillet with no-stick cooking spray and set aside.

Start by putting handle end of spoon in center of dough and "degas, pull and stretch" dough to form a ball.

Generously dust dough and side of bowl with flour... roll dough in flour to coat. Roll dough out of bowl into proofing skillet.

Place proofing skillet in a warm draft-free location, cover with a lint-free towel, and proof for 1 to 2 hours.

1 to 2 hours later

Before dough is fully proofed... move rack to lower third of oven, place baking vessel in oven, and pre-heat to 450 degrees F.

When oven has come to temperature...

Remove baking vessel from oven, transfer dough from proofing skillet to baking vessel, score (optional) and bake for 40 minutes with the top on and 3 to 15 minutes with the top off depending on how rustic (hard) you like your crust.

40 to 55 minutes later

Gently turn loaf out on work surface and place on cooling rack.

Classic White Bread (standard bread pan)

You can make classic white bread using the no-knead method. Think about it. There are two basic steps to making bread... you make the dough... you bake the bread. And these two steps are independent of each other. Therefore... if you have been kneading your dough to make classic white bread, you can replace the kneading process with the no-knead method, then bake your bread just as you did in the past.

YouTube Video In Support of Recipe: <u>Introduction to Baking No-Knead Bread in Bread Pans</u> (video released prior to new technique)

Classic White Bread

Pour water into a 3 to 4 qt glass mixing bowl.

<u>14 oz cool tap Water</u>

Add salt and yeast... give a quick stir to combine.

<u>2 tsp Salt</u>

<u>1/2 tsp Instant Yeast</u>

Add flour... stir until dough forms a shaggy ball, then tumble dough to combine moist flour on the bottom with dry flour, scrape flour from side of bowl and finish combining.

<u>3-1/2 cups Bread Flour</u>

Cover bowl with plastic wrap, place in a warm draft-free location, and proof for 8 to 24 hours.

8 to 24 hours later (standard bread pan)

When dough has risen and developed its gluten structure... spray an 8-1/2" x 4-1/2" bread pan with no-stick cooking spray and set aside.

Start by putting handle end of spoon in center of dough and "degas, pull and stretch" dough to form a ball.

Generously dust dough and side of bowl with flour... roll dough in flour to coat. Roll dough out of bowl into bread pan.

Place pan in a warm draft-free location, cover with a lint-free towel, and proof for 1 to 2 hours.

1 to 2 hours later

Before dough is fully proofed... move oven rack to the middle of the oven and pre-heat to 400 degrees F.

When oven has come to temperature

Place loaf pan in the oven and bake for 45 minutes.

45 minutes later

Gently turn loaf out on to the work surface and place on a cooling rack (cooling racks allow the bottom of the loaf to air dry).

Cheddar Cheese Bread (Dutch oven)

Bread is one of the great comfort foods. Fresh from the oven bread is something special... add cheese and you have a winner. Something your friends and guests will love. This is a remarkably simple recipe that is as delicious as it looks. I used a 3 qt *Lodge* Enameled cast iron Dutch oven to shape this loaf.

Cheddar Cheese Bread

Pour water into a 3 to 4 qt glass mixing bowl.

> 13-1/2 oz cool tap Water

Add salt and yeast... give a quick stir to combine.

> 1-1/2 tsp Salt
> 1/4 tsp Instant Yeast

Add flour... then cheese. Stir until dough forms a shaggy ball, then tumble dough to combine moist flour on the bottom with dry flour, scrape flour from side of bowl and finish combining.

> 3 cups Bread Flour
> 1 cup coarse shredded Cheddar Cheese

Cover bowl with plastic wrap, place in a warm draft-free location, and proof for 8 to 24 hours.

8 to 24 hours later (Dutch oven)

When dough has risen and developed its gluten structure... spray an 8" proofing skillet with no-stick cooking spray and set aside.

Start by putting handle end of spoon in center of dough and "degas, pull and stretch" dough to form a ball.

Garnish... sprinkle dough ball with cheese and roll to coat.

> 1/4 cup coarse shredded Cheddar Cheese

Generously dust dough and side of bowl with flour... roll dough in flour to coat. Roll dough out of bowl into proofing skillet.

Place proofing skillet in a warm draft-free location, cover with a lint-free towel, and proof for 1 to 2 hours.

1 to 2 hours later

Before dough is fully proofed... move rack to lower third of oven, place baking vessel in oven, and pre-heat to 450 degrees F.

When oven has come to temperature...

Remove baking vessel from oven and transfer dough from proofing skillet to baking vessel.

Sprinkle a little cheese on top (a little extra garnish).

> Pinch coarse shredded Cheddar Cheese

Score (optional) and bake for 30 minutes with the top on and 3 to 15 minutes with the top off depending on how rustic (hard) you like your crust.

30 to 45 minutes later

Gently turn loaf out on work surface and place on cooling rack.

Cinnamon Raisin Bread (long covered baker)

Homemade fresh from the oven cinnamon raisin bread is a great way to start your day and when our guests stay overnight, my wife wants them to wake up to the aroma of fresh for the oven cinnamon raisin bread filling the house. I used a *Sassafras* superstone oblong covered baker to shape this loaf.

Notes: Because cinnamon retards yeast activity... this recipe requires additional yeast (1 tsp) and a longer first proofing (minimum of 12 hours). And I don't bake it with the top off... the bread will be dark brown after 30 minutes because of the ingredients (cinnamon and brown sugar) and I'm not looking for a hard rustic crust.

Cinnamon Raisin Bread

Pour water into a 3 to 4 qt glass mixing bowl.

14-1/2 oz cool tap Water

Add salt, yeast, sugar, and cinnamon... use a whisk or fork to combine.

1-1/2 tsp Salt

1 tsp Instant Yeast

2 Tbsp Brown Sugar

1 Tbsp ground Cinnamon

Add flour... then raisins. Stir until dough forms a shaggy ball, then tumble dough to combine moist flour on the bottom with dry flour, scrape flour from side of bowl and finish combining.

3 cups Bread Flour

1 cup Raisins

Cover bowl with plastic wrap, place in a warm draft-free location, and proof for 12 to 24 hours.

12 to 24 hours later (long baker)

When dough has risen and developed its gluten structure... spray an 8" proofing skillet with no-stick cooking spray and set aside.

Start by putting handle end of spoon in center of dough and "degas, pull and stretch" dough to form a ball.

Generously dust dough and side of bowl with flour... roll dough in flour to coat. Roll dough out of bowl into proofing skillet.

Place proofing skillet in a warm draft-free location, cover with a lint-free towel, and proof for 1 to 2 hours.

1 to 2 hours later

Before dough is fully proofed... move rack to lower third of oven, place baking vessel in oven, and pre-heat to 450 degrees F.

When oven has come to temperature...

Remove baking vessel from oven, transfer dough from proofing skillet to baking vessel, score (optional) and bake for 30 minutes with the top on.

30 minutes later

Gently turn loaf out on work surface and place on cooling rack.

Cinnamon Raisin Swirl Bread (long covered baker)

This is bread your family and friends will love. It has a unique look and great taste. It's the perfect bread for your morning toast. I used a *Sassafras* superstone oblong covered baker to shape this loaf.

Pour water into a 3 to 4 qt glass mixing bowl.

    <u>14 oz cool tap Water</u>

Add salt, yeast, and sugar... give a quick stir to combine.

    <u>1-1/2 tsp Salt</u>

    <u>1/4 tsp Instant Yeast</u>

    <u>1 Tbsp Sugar</u>

Add flour... stir until dough forms a shaggy ball, then tumble dough to combine moist flour on the bottom with dry flour, scrape flour from side of bowl and finish combining.

    <u>3 cups Bread Flour</u>

Cover bowl with plastic wrap, place in a warm draft-free location, and proof for 8 to 24 hours.

8 to 24 hours later (long covered baker)

When the dough has risen and developed its gluten structure... set a long loaf pan (12" x 4-1/2") and a sheet of parchment paper off to the side (I use a long loaf pan lined with parchment paper as a proofing vessel to pre-shape the loaf).

Prep... put sugar in bowl, add cinnamon, stir to combine, and set aside.

    <u>1/4 cup White Sugar</u>

    <u>1 level tsp Cinnamon</u>

Place a silicone pad on the work surface and lightly dust with flour (I like to use a silicone pad as a work surface when the dough needs to be rolled to shape).

Start by putting handle end of spoon in center of dough and "degas, pull and stretch" dough to form a ball.

Generously dust dough and side of bowl with flour... roll dough in flour to coat.

Roll dough (and excess flour) out of bowl onto silicone pad.

Press lightly to flatten and spread... then drizzle with vegetable oil and use a rolling pin to spread the oil. Then turn the dough over so that the oil side is on the silicone pad (a little layer of oil on the bottom will make it easier to roll and spread the dough... and keep it from sticking).

<u>Vegetable Oil for drizzling</u>

Drizzle top with a little oil and roll dough into a rectangle 12' wide and as long as possible (thinner will give you more swirls).

Sprinkle dough with cinnamon-sugar mixture and spread with your hand.

Distribute raisins evenly.

<u>1 cup Raisins</u>

Start at the 12" end and roll the dough into a log (use a plastic bowl scraper to slide under the dough to assist with any sticking).

Place dough in the center of the parchment paper seam side down and use the parchment paper as a sling to carry dough to the loaf pan for proofing.

Place pan in a warm draft-free location, cover with a lint-free towel, and proof for 1 to 2 hours.

1 to 2 hours later

Before dough is fully proofed... move rack to lower third of oven, place baking vessel in oven, and pre-heat to 450 degrees F.

When oven has come to temperature...

Remove baking vessel from oven, use the parchment paper as a sling to transfer dough from proofing pan to baking vessel, and bake for 30 minutes with the top on and 3 to 5 minutes with the top off.

30 to 35 minutes later

Gently turn loaf out on work surface and place on cooling rack.

Beer Bread (Dutch oven)

The purpose of this recipe is to introduce those of you who make beer bread to the no-knead method of making dough and introduce those of you who make no-knead bread to beer bread. One simple recipe with hundreds of options... simply by changing the wet ingredient—the beer—from a lager, to an amber, or a hefeweizen you can have a new and uniquely flavored bread. It's fun to experiment with ingredients. The beer isle is full of ideas.

Do you like the shape of the loaf in the picture? I achieved it by using our 2.6 qt *Emile Henry* ceramic Dutch oven. Because of its smaller size (8" diameter) when the loaf couldn't expand width-wise, it expanded height-wise, which gave me this beautiful round boule. It's fun to experiment with shapes.

Beer Bread

Pour beer into a 3 to 4 qt glass mixing bowl.

<u>12 oz room temperature Beer</u>

Add salt and yeast... give a quick stir to combine.

<u>1-1/2 tsp Salt</u>

<u>1/4 tsp Instant Yeast</u>

Add flour... stir until dough forms a shaggy ball, then tumble dough to combine moist flour on the bottom with dry flour, scrape flour from side of bowl and finish combining.

<u>3 cups Bread Flour</u>

Cover bowl with plastic wrap, place in a warm draft-free location, and proof for 8 to 24 hours.

8 to 24 hours later (Dutch oven)

When dough has risen and developed its gluten structure... spray an 8" proofing skillet with no-stick cooking spray and set aside.

Start by putting handle end of spoon in center of dough and "degas, pull and stretch" dough to form a ball.

Generously dust dough and side of bowl with flour... roll dough in flour to coat. Roll dough out of bowl into proofing skillet.

Place proofing skillet in a warm draft-free location, cover with a lint-free towel, and proof for 1 to 2 hours.

1 to 2 hours later

Before dough is fully proofed... move rack to lower third of oven, place baking vessel in oven, and pre-heat to 450 degrees F.

When oven has come to temperature...

Remove baking vessel from oven, transfer dough from proofing skillet to baking vessel, score (optional) and bake for 30 minutes with the top on and 3 to 15 minutes with the top off depending on how rustic (hard) you like your crust.

30 to 45 minutes later

Gently turn loaf out on work surface and place on cooling rack.

Buttermilk Bread (long covered baker)

If you like ranch dressing... you like buttermilk. And this isn't the average Buttermilk bread... this is an artisan buttermilk bread with an airy crumb and tender crust. The appearance is excellent and the taste is great. Buttermilk is a great all-purpose bread. Buttermilk gives it a rich tangy flavor with a subtle buttery depth that is great for sandwiches and toast.

It is a common misconception to associate buttermilk with the richness of butter... buttermilk does not have butterfat. Buttermilk is the liquid remaining after taking the fat out from the milk in the process of making butter, thus it is lower in calories and fat than butter and higher in calcium, Vitamin B12 and potassium than regular milk. And it's important to use cultured buttermilk, if you substitute 2% for cultured buttermilk in this recipe it will upset the balance of wet and dry ingredients (it's thinner), and you don't want to lose the nutritional value of buttermilk. After all, you wouldn't want to take the "yo" out of yogurt.

I used our *Sassafras* superstone oblong covered baker to shape this loaf.

Buttermilk Bread

Pour buttermilk and water into a 3 to 4 qt glass mixing bowl.

<u>8 oz Cultured Buttermilk</u>
<u>6 oz cool tap Water</u>

Add salt, yeast, sugar and oil... give a quick stir to combine.

<u>1-1/2 tsp Salt</u>
<u>1/4 tsp Instant Yeast</u>
<u>1 Tbsp Sugar</u>
<u>1 Tbsp Vegetable Oil</u>

Add flour... stir until dough forms a shaggy ball, then tumble dough to combine moist flour on the bottom with dry flour, scrape flour from side of bowl and finish combining.

<u>3 cups Bread Flour</u>

Cover bowl with plastic wrap, place in a warm draft-free location, and proof for 8 to 24 hours.

8 to 24 hours later (long covered baker)

When dough has risen and developed its gluten structure... spray an 8" proofing skillet with no-stick cooking spray and set aside.

Start by putting handle end of spoon in center of dough and "degas, pull and stretch" dough to form a ball.

Generously dust dough and side of bowl with flour... roll dough in flour to coat. Roll dough out of bowl into proofing skillet.

Place proofing skillet in a warm draft-free location, cover with a lint-free towel, and proof for 1 to 2 hours.

1 to 2 hours later

Before dough is fully proofed... move rack to lower third of oven, place baking vessel in oven, and pre-heat to 450 degrees F.

When oven has come to temperature...

Remove baking vessel from oven, transfer dough from proofing skillet to baking vessel, score (optional) and bake for 30 minutes with the top on and 1+ minutes with the top off.

30 to 35 minutes later

Gently turn loaf out on work surface and place on cooling rack.

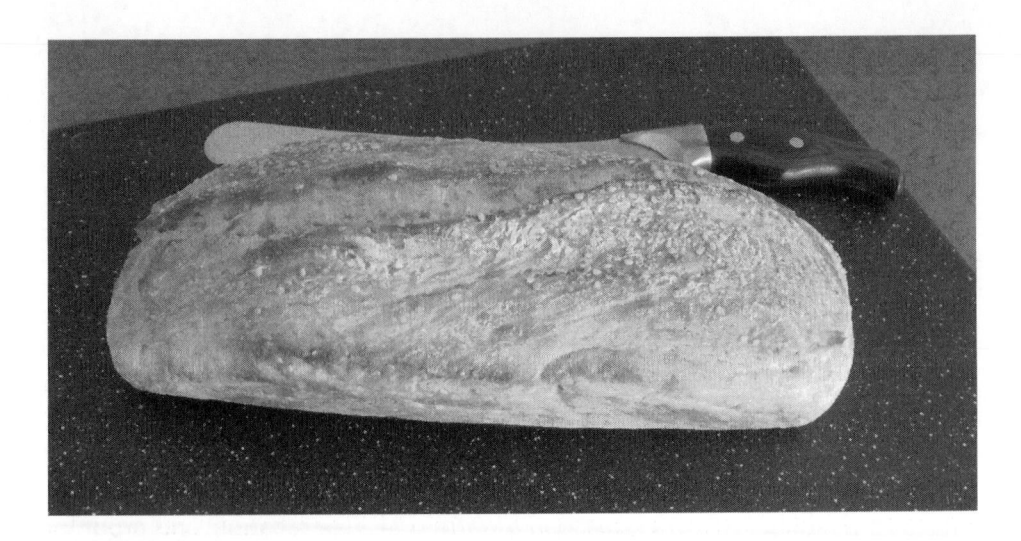

Semolina Bread (long covered baker + garnish)

Semolina is a very fine textured flour made from durum wheat and frequently used to make pasta. It gives bread a golden hue with a distinct flavor and the sesame seeds provide a mild undertone of flavor as it gives the bread its beautiful appearance. I used our *Sassafras* superstone oblong covered baker to shape this loaf.

Semolina Bread

Pour water into a 3 to 4 qt glass mixing bowl.

> 15 oz cool tap Water

Add salt, yeast, seeds and olive oil... give a quick stir to combine.

> 1-1/2 tsp Salt
> 1/4 tsp Instant Yeast
> 2 Tbsp Sesame Seeds
> 1 Tbsp Olive Oil

Add flour... stir until dough forms a shaggy ball, then tumble dough to combine moist flour on the bottom with dry flour, scrape flour from side of bowl and finish combining.

> 2-1/2 cups Bread Flour
> 1 cup Semolina Flour

Cover bowl with plastic wrap, place in a warm draft-free location, and proof for 8 to 24 hours.

8 to 24 hours later (long covered baker + garnish)

When dough has risen and developed its gluten structure... spray an 8" proofing skillet with no-stick cooking spray and set aside.

Start by putting handle end of spoon in center of dough and "degas, pull and stretch" dough to form a ball.

Garnish... sprinkle dough ball with sesame seed and roll to coat.

> 2 Tbsp Sesame Seeds

Generously dust dough and side of bowl with flour... roll dough in flour to coat.

Roll dough out of bowl into proofing skillet.

Place proofing skillet in a warm draft-free location, cover with a lint-free towel, and proof for 1 to 2 hours.

1 to 2 hours later

Before dough is fully proofed... move rack to lower third of oven, place baking vessel in oven, and pre-heat to 450 degrees F.

When oven has come to temperature...

Remove baking vessel from oven, transfer dough from proofing skillet to baking vessel, score (optional) and bake for 30 minutes with the top on and 3 to 5 minutes with the top off.

30 to 35 minutes later

Gently turn loaf out on work surface and place on cooling rack.

Sesame Seed Bread (Dutch oven + garnish & baste)

Garnishing and basting can give bread a very appetizing appearance. This recipe was updated to include the new technique for basting and garnishing. I used our 2.6 qt *Emile Henry* flame top ceramic Dutch oven to shape this loaf.

Sesame Seed Bread

Pour water into a 3 to 4 qt glass mixing bowl.

> 12 oz cool tap Water

Add salt, yeast, seeds and oil... give a quick stir to combine.

> 1-1/2 tsp Salt
> 1/4 tsp Instant Yeast
> 1/3 cup Sesame Seeds
> 1 Tbsp Flax Seeds
> 1 Tbsp Vegetable Oil

Add flour... stir until dough forms a shaggy ball, then tumble dough to combine moist flour on the bottom with dry flour, scrape flour from side of bowl and finish combining.

> 3 cups Bread Flour

Cover bowl with plastic wrap, place in a warm draft-free location, and proof for 8 to 24 hours.

8 to 24 hours later (Dutch oven + garnish & baste)

When dough has risen and developed its gluten structure... spray an 8" proofing skillet with no-stick cooking spray and set aside.

Start by putting handle end of spoon in center of dough and "degas, pull and stretch" dough to form a ball.

Garnish... sprinkle dough ball with seeds and roll to coat.

> 2 Tbsp Sesame Seeds
> 1 tsp Flax Seeds

Baste... place 1 egg yolk in a small mixing bowl, add water, and whip to combine. Then pour egg wash into proofing skillet, swirl to coat skillet and discard excess.

> 1 Egg Yolk
> Splash of Water

Roll dough out of bowl into proofing skillet.

Place proofing skillet in a warm draft-free location, cover with a lint-free towel, and proof for 1 to 2 hours.

1 to 2 hours later

Before dough is fully proofed... move rack to lower third of oven, place baking vessel in oven, and pre-heat to 450 degrees F.

When oven has come to temperature...

Remove baking vessel from oven, transfer dough from proofing skillet to baking vessel (invert so that garnished and basted bottom is on top), score (optional) and bake for 30 minutes with the top on and 3 to 15 minutes with the top off depending on how rustic (hard) you like your crust.

30 to 45 minutes later

Gently turn loaf out on work surface and place on cooling rack.

Honey Oatmeal Bread (Dutch oven + garnish)

Fresh from the oven bread with the wholesome goodness of oats and the sweetness of honey... what's not to like? This loaf is as delicious to eat as it is pleasing to the eye. I use the "roll to coat" method to garnish and a 3 qt *Lodge* Enameled cast iron Dutch oven to shape this loaf.

Honey Oatmeal Bread

Pour water into a 3 to 4 qt glass mixing bowl.

> 14 oz cool tap Water

Add salt, yeast and honey... give a quick stir to combine.

> 1-1/2 tsp Salt
>
> 1/4 tsp Instant Yeast
>
> 2 Tbsp Honey

Add flour... then oats (if oats are added before flour they will absorb the water and it will be harder to combine)... stir until dough forms a shaggy ball, tumble to absorb remaining flour, scrape flour from side of bowl and finish combining.

> 3 cups Bread Flour
>
> 1 cup Old Fashioned Quaker Oats

Cover bowl with plastic wrap, place in a warm draft-free location, and proof for 8 to 24 hours.

8 to 24 hours later (Dutch oven + garnish)

When dough has risen and developed its gluten structure... spray an 8" proofing skillet with no-stick cooking spray and set aside.

Start by putting handle end of spoon in center of dough and "degas, pull and stretch" dough to form a ball.

Garnish... sprinkle dough ball with oats and roll to coat.

> 1/4 cup Old Fashioned Quaker Oats

Generously dust dough and side of bowl with flour... roll dough in flour to coat. Roll dough out of bowl into proofing skillet.

Place proofing skillet in a warm draft-free location, cover with a lint-free towel, and proof for 1 to 2 hours.

1 to 2 hours later

Before dough is fully proofed... move rack to lower third of oven, place baking vessel in oven, and pre-heat to 450 degrees F.

When oven has come to temperature...

Remove baking vessel from oven, transfer dough from proofing skillet to baking vessel, score (optional) and bake for 30 minutes with the top on and 3 to 15 minutes with the top off depending on how rustic (hard) you like your crust.

30 to 45 minutes later

Gently turn loaf out on work surface and place on cooling rack.

Multigrain Country White Bread (Dutch oven)

This is one of my most popular loaves. My first multigrain loaves used 2 cups bread flour and 1 cup wheat flour. One time I forgot the wheat flour and used 3 cups bread flour. Surprise, surprise... the multigrain country white became one of my most requested breads. I had assumed those who like grains also like wheat breads, but there appears to be a significant segment of our society who likes multigrain bread without the wheat bread taste. Wheat is one of those things you either like or don't like, but it doesn't mean you don't like multigrain bread. I used a 2.6 qt *Emile Henry* flame top ceramic Dutch oven to shape this loaf.

Multigrain Country White Bread

Pour water into a 3 to 4 qt glass mixing bowl.

> 14 oz cool tap Water

Add salt, yeast and seeds... give a quick stir to combine.

> 1-1/2 tsp Salt
> 1/4 tsp Instant Yeast
> 1 Tbsp Sesame Seeds
> 1 Tbsp Flax Seeds

Add flour... then oats (if oats are added before flour they will absorb the water and it will be harder to combine)... stir until dough forms a shaggy ball, tumble to absorb remaining flour, scrape flour from side of bowl and finish combining.

> 3 cups Bread Flour
> 1/2 cup Old Fashioned Quaker Oats

Cover bowl with plastic wrap, place in a warm draft-free location, and proof for 8 to 24 hours.

8 to 24 hours later (Dutch oven)

When dough has risen and developed its gluten structure... spray an 8" proofing skillet with no-stick cooking spray and set aside.

Start by putting handle end of spoon in center of dough and "degas, pull and stretch" dough to form a ball.

Garnish... sprinkle dough ball with grains and roll to coat.

> 2 Tbsp Old Fashioned Quaker Oats

Generously dust dough and side of bowl with flour... roll dough in flour to coat.

Roll dough out of bowl into proofing skillet.

Place proofing skillet in a warm draft-free location, cover with a lint-free towel, and proof for 1 to 2 hours.

1 to 2 hours later

Before dough is fully proofed... move rack to lower third of oven, place baking vessel in oven, and pre-heat to 450 degrees F.

When oven has come to temperature...

Remove baking vessel from oven, transfer dough from proofing skillet to baking vessel, score (optional) and bake for 30 minutes with the top on and 3 to 15 minutes with the top off depending on how rustic (hard) you like your crust.

30 to 45 minutes later

Gently turn loaf out on work surface and place on cooling rack.

Harvest 8 Grain Country White Bread (Dutch oven + garnish)

This Harvest 8 Grain White Bread has a more robust and complex flavor than the Multigrain Country White Bread. I experimented with and tested a number of my own multigrain mixtures before I discovered King Arthur's Harvest Grains Blend and—as they state on their website—the whole oat berries, millet, rye flakes and wheat flakes enhance texture while the flax, poppy, sesame, and sunflower seeds add crunch and great, nutty flavor. Wow, the flavor is great... and it's a lot easier and more practical to purchase a blend of seeds. I used a 2.6 qt *Emile Henry* flame top ceramic Dutch oven to shape this loaf.

Notes: I try not to be brand specific in my recipes, but I did not want to give my subscribers and readers a list of 8 grains to buy. Both the cost and availability could be a problem, so I used King Arthur's Harvest Grains Blend, but you may want to try a blend that is available at your local health food store. It's part of the fun of being your own baker.

Pour water into a 3 to 4 qt glass mixing bowl.

<u>13 oz cool tap Water</u>

Add salt, yeast and seeds... give a quick stir to combine.

<u>1-1/2 tsp Salt</u>

<u>1/4 tsp Instant Yeast</u>

<u>2/3 cup King Arthur Harvest Grains Blend</u>

Add flour... stir until dough forms a shaggy ball, then tumble dough to combine moist flour on the bottom with dry flour, scrape flour from side of bowl and finish combining.

<u>3 cups Bread Flour</u>

Cover bowl with plastic wrap, place in a warm draft-free location, and proof for 8 to 24 hours.

8 to 24 hours later (Dutch oven + garnish)

When dough has risen and developed its gluten structure... spray an 8" proofing skillet with no-stick cooking spray and set aside.

Start by putting handle end of spoon in center of dough and "degas, pull and stretch" dough to form a ball.

Garnish... sprinkle dough ball with grains and roll to coat.

<u>2 Tbsp King Arthur Harvest Grains Blend</u>

Generously dust dough and side of bowl with flour... roll dough in flour to coat. Roll dough out of bowl into proofing skillet.

Place proofing skillet in a warm draft-free location, cover with a lint-free towel, and proof for 1 to 2 hours.

1 to 2 hours later

Before dough is fully proofed... move rack to lower third of oven, place baking vessel in oven, and pre-heat to 450 degrees F.

When oven has come to temperature...

Remove baking vessel from oven, transfer dough from proofing skillet to baking vessel, score (optional) and bake for 30 minutes with the top on and 3 to 15 minutes with the top off depending on how rustic (hard) you like your crust.

30 to 45 minutes later

Gently turn loaf out on work surface and place on cooling rack.

Honey Whole Wheat Bread (Dutch oven)

This whole wheat recipe balances the nutrition and nutty taste of whole wheat with the crumb of a Country White in a hearty, moist, faintly sweet loaf with a touch of honey. Whole wheat is a very easy bread to make. I like to score the top with an "X" and baked it in a smaller 2.6 qt Dutch oven which gives me a nice artisan look. I use our 2.6 qt *Emile Henry* ceramic Dutch oven to shape this loaf.

Honey Whole Wheat Bread

Pour water into a 3 to 4 qt glass mixing bowl.

> 13 oz cool tap Water

Add salt, yeast, oil and honey... give a quick stir to combine.

> 1-1/2 tsp Salt
> 1/4 tsp Instant Yeast
> 1 Tbsp Vegetable Oil
> 1 Tbsp Honey

Add flour... stir until dough forms a shaggy ball, then tumble dough to combine moist flour on the bottom with dry flour, scrape flour from side of bowl and finish combining.

> 1-1/2 cups Bread Flour
> 1-1/2 cups Whole Wheat Flour

Cover bowl with plastic wrap, place in a warm draft-free location, and proof for 8 to 24 hours.

8 to 24 hours later (Dutch oven)

When dough has risen and developed its gluten structure... spray an 8" proofing skillet with no-stick cooking spray and set aside.

Start by putting handle end of spoon in center of dough and "degas, pull and stretch" dough to form a ball.

Generously dust dough and side of bowl with flour... roll dough in flour to coat. Roll dough out of bowl into proofing skillet.

Place proofing skillet in a warm draft-free location, cover with a lint-free towel, and proof for 1 to 2 hours.

1 to 2 hours later

Before dough is fully proofed... move rack to lower third of oven, place baking vessel in oven, and pre-heat to 450 degrees F.

When oven has come to temperature...

Remove baking vessel from oven, transfer dough from proofing skillet to baking vessel, score (optional) and bake for 30 minutes with the top on and 3 to 15 minutes with the top off depending on how rustic (hard) you like your crust.

30 to 45 minutes later

Gently turn loaf out on work surface and place on cooling rack.

Multigrain Whole Wheat Bread (Dutch oven)

This is very similar to the Multigrain Country White, except with the wheat flour. It's intended to be a simple loaf with broad general appeal. If you haven't ever made wheat bread before and you like the texture of grain, this is an excellent choice for your first loaf. Simple recipe... simple flavors... universally pleasing taste. I used a higher percentage of bread flour which gives this loaf a little better crumb. I used our *Le Creuset* 2.25 qt eggplant Dutch oven to shape this loaf.

Multigrain Whole Wheat Bread

Pour water into a 3 to 4 qt glass mixing bowl.

> 15 oz cool tap Water

Add salt, yeast, sugar, seeds, and olive oil... give a quick stir to combine.

> 1-1/2 tsp Salt
>
> 1/4 tsp Instant Yeast
>
> 1 Tbsp Sugar
>
> 1 Tbsp Sesame Seeds
>
> 1 Tbsp Flax Seeds
>
> 1 Tbsp extra-virgin Olive Oil

Add flour... then oats (if oats are added before flour they will absorb the water and it will be harder to combine)... stir until dough forms a shaggy ball, tumble to absorb remaining flour, scrape flour from side of bowl and finish combining.

> 2 cups Bread Flour
>
> 1 cup Whole Wheat Flour
>
> 1 cup Old Fashioned Quaker Oats

Cover bowl with plastic wrap, place in a warm draft-free location, and proof for 8 to 24 hours.

8 to 24 hours later (Dutch oven)

When dough has risen and developed its gluten structure... spray an 8" proofing skillet with no-stick cooking spray and set aside.

Start by putting handle end of spoon in center of dough and "degas, pull and stretch" dough to form a ball.

Generously dust dough and side of bowl with flour... roll dough in flour to coat. Roll dough out of bowl into proofing skillet.

Place proofing skillet in a warm draft-free location, cover with a lint-free towel, and proof for 1 to 2 hours.

1 to 2 hours later

Before dough is fully proofed... move rack to lower third of oven, place baking vessel in oven, and pre-heat to 450 degrees F.

When oven has come to temperature...

Remove baking vessel from oven, transfer dough from proofing skillet to baking vessel, score (optional) and bake for 30 minutes with the top on and 3 to 15 minutes with the top off depending on how rustic (hard) you like your crust.

30 to 45 minutes later

Gently turn loaf out on work surface and place on cooling rack.

Sunflower Seed & Honey Whole Wheat (Dutch oven + garnish & baste)
The sweetness of honey with sunflower seeds... a beautiful loaf that is sure to please. I used a 3 qt *Lodge* Enameled cast iron Dutch oven to shape this loaf.

Sunflower Seed & Honey Whole Wheat Bread

Pour water into a 3 to 4 qt glass mixing bowl.

12 oz cool tap Water

Add salt, yeast, honey, seeds and oil... give a quick stir to combine.

1-1/2 tsp Salt

1/4 tsp Instant Yeast

1 Tbsp Vegetable Oil

2 Tbsp Honey

1/3 cup Sunflower Seeds

Add flour... stir until dough forms a shaggy ball, then tumble dough to combine moist flour on the bottom with dry flour, scrape flour from side of bowl and finish combining.

2 cups Bread Flour

1 cup Whole Wheat Flour

Cover bowl with plastic wrap, place in a warm draft-free location, and proof for 8 to 24 hours.

8 to 24 hours later (Dutch oven + garnish & baste)

When dough has risen and developed its gluten structure... spray an 8" proofing skillet with no-stick cooking spray and set aside.

Start by putting handle end of spoon in center of dough and "degas, pull and stretch" dough to form a ball.

Garnish... sprinkle dough ball with seeds and roll to coat.

2 Tbsp Sunflower Seeds

Baste... place 1 egg yolk in a small mixing bowl, add water, and whip to combine. Then pour egg wash into proofing skillet, swirl to coat skillet and discard excess.

1 Egg Yolk

Splash of Water

Roll dough out of bowl into proofing skillet.

Place proofing skillet in a warm draft-free location, cover with a lint-free towel, and proof for 1 to 2 hours.

1 to 2 hours later

Before dough is fully proofed... move rack to lower third of oven, place baking vessel in oven, and pre-heat to 450 degrees F.

When oven has come to temperature...

Remove baking vessel from oven, transfer dough from proofing skillet to baking vessel (invert so that garnished and basted bottom is on top), score (optional) and bake for 30 minutes with the top on and 3 to 15 minutes with the top off depending on how rustic (hard) you like your crust.

30 to 45 minutes later

Gently turn loaf out on work surface and place on cooling rack.

Honey Granola Whole Wheat Bread (Dutch oven)

This is for those of you who like granola... a nice wheat bread with granola and a hint of honey. I used our *Emile Henry* 2.6 qt ceramic Dutch oven to shape this loaf.

Honey Granola Whole Wheat Bread

Pour water into a 3 to 4 qt glass mixing bowl.

14 oz cool tap Water

Add salt, yeast, oil, honey and granola... give a quick stir to combine.

1-1/2 tsp Salt

1/4 tsp Instant Yeast

1 Tbsp Vegetable Oil

1 Tbsp Honey

3 (1.5 oz) Granola Bars (diced into 1/4" cubes)

Add flour... stir until dough forms a shaggy ball, then tumble dough to combine moist flour on the bottom with dry flour, scrape flour from side of bowl and finish combining.

2 cups Bread Flour

1 cup Whole Wheat Flour

Cover bowl with plastic wrap, place in a warm draft-free location, and proof for 8 to 24 hours.

8 to 24 hours later (Dutch oven)

When dough has risen and developed its gluten structure... spray an 8" proofing skillet with no-stick cooking spray and set aside.

Start by putting handle end of spoon in center of dough and "degas, pull and stretch" dough to form a ball.

Generously dust dough and side of bowl with flour... roll dough in flour to coat.

Roll dough out of bowl into proofing skillet.

Place proofing skillet in a warm draft-free location, cover with a lint-free towel, and proof for 1 to 2 hours.

1 to 2 hours later

Before dough is fully proofed... move rack to lower third of oven, place baking vessel in oven, and pre-heat to 450 degrees F.

When oven has come to temperature...

Remove baking vessel from oven, transfer dough from proofing skillet to baking vessel, score (optional) and bake for 30 minutes with the top on and 3 to 15 minutes with the top off depending on how rustic (hard) you like your crust.

30 to 45 minutes later

Gently turn loaf out on work surface and place on cooling rack.

Harvest 8 Grain Whole Wheat Bread (Dutch oven + garnish & baste)

This Harvest 8 Grain Wheat Bread has a more robust and complex flavor than the multigrain country white and wheat breads. I experimented with and tested a number of my own multigrain mixtures before I discovered King Arthur's Harvest Grains Blend and—as they state on their website—the whole oat berries, millet, rye flakes and wheat flakes enhance texture while the flax, poppy, sesame, and sunflower seeds add crunch and great, nutty flavor. Wow, the flavor is great... and it's a lot easier and more practical to purchase a blend of seeds. I used our *Le Creuset* 2.25 qt eggplant Dutch oven to shape this loaf.

Harvest 8 Grain Whole Wheat Bread

Pour water into a 3 to 4 qt glass mixing bowl.

> 14 oz cool tap Water

Add salt, yeast, sugar, grains and olive oil... give a quick stir to combine.

> 1-1/2 tsp Salt
> 1/4 tsp Instant Yeast
> 1 Tbsp Sugar
> 2/3 cup King Arthur Harvest Grains Blend
> 1 Tbsp extra-virgin Olive Oil

Add flour... stir until dough forms a shaggy ball, then tumble dough to combine moist flour on the bottom with dry flour, scrape flour from side of bowl and finish combining.

> 2 cups Bread Flour
> 1 cup Whole Wheat Flour

Cover bowl with plastic wrap, place in a warm draft-free location, and proof for 8 to 24 hours.

8 to 24 hours later (Dutch oven + garnish & baste)

When dough has risen and developed its gluten structure... spray an 8" proofing skillet with no-stick cooking spray and set aside.

Start by putting handle end of spoon in center of dough and "degas, pull and stretch" dough to form a ball.

Garnish... sprinkle dough ball with grains and roll to coat.

> 2 Tbsp King Arthur Harvest Grains Blend

Baste... place 1 egg yolk in a small mixing bowl, add water, and whip to combine. Then pour egg wash into proofing skillet, swirl to coat skillet and discard excess.

> 1 Egg Yolk
> Splash of Water

Roll dough out of bowl into proofing skillet.

Place proofing skillet in a warm draft-free location, cover with a lint-free towel, and proof for 1 to 2 hours.

1 to 2 hours later

Before dough is fully proofed... move rack to lower third of oven, place baking vessel in oven, and pre-heat to 450 degrees F.

When oven has come to temperature...

Remove baking vessel from oven, transfer dough from proofing skillet to baking vessel (invert so that garnished and basted bottom is on top), score (optional) and bake for 30 minutes with the top on and 3 to 15 minutes with the top off depending on how rustic (hard) you like your crust.

30 to 45 minutes later

Gently turn loaf out on work surface and place on cooling rack.

Caraway Rye Bread (long covered baker)

This is a rustic rye bread with a mild rye flavor and a generous amount of caraway seeds. Rye bread remains very popular throughout the Mediterranean and is the perfect complement to corned beef and pastrami. I used our *Sassafras* superstone long covered baker to bake these loaves.

Caraway Rye Bread

Pour water into a 3 to 4 qt glass mixing bowl.

13 oz cool tap Water

Add salt, yeast, sugar, seeds and olive oil... give a quick stir to combine.

1-1/2 tsp Salt

1/4 tsp Instant Yeast

1 Tbsp Sugar

2 Tbsp Caraway Seeds

1 Tbsp extra-virgin Olive Oil

Add flour... stir until dough forms a shaggy ball, then tumble dough to combine moist flour on the bottom with dry flour, scrape flour from side of bowl and finish combining.

2 cups Bread Flour

1 cup Rye Flour

Cover bowl with plastic wrap, place in a warm draft-free location, and proof for 8 to 24 hours.

8 to 24 hours later (half loaves – long covered baker)

When dough has risen and developed its gluten structure... set two 10" x 12" sheets of parchment paper off to the set aside.

Start by putting handle end of spoon in center of dough and "degas, pull and stretch" dough to form a ball.

Generously dust dough and side of bowl with flour... roll dough in flour to coat.

Roll dough (and excess flour) out of bowl onto work surface.

Divide dough into 2 portions.

Then (one portion at a time) roll dough on work surface (dusting with flour as needed), form a long loaf, and place on parchment paper.

Place dough in a warm draft-free location, cover with a lint-free towel, and proof for 1 to 2 hours.

1 to 2 hours later

Before dough is fully proofed... move rack to lower third of oven, place baking vessel in oven, and pre-heat to 450 degrees F.

When oven has come to temperature...

Remove baking vessel from oven, use the parchment paper as a sling to lift the dough up and place it in the baking vessel, score (optional) and bake for 25 minutes with the top on and 3 minutes with the top off.

30 to 45 minutes later

Gently turn loaf out on work surface and place on cooling rack. Repeat process for second half loaf.

Harvest 9 Grain Rye Bread (Dutch oven)

This hearty and healthy bread combines rye flour, caraway seeds and a blend of harvest grains into one wonderful loaf that is sure to please. I used our *Le Creuset* 2.25 qt eggplant Dutch oven to shape this loaf.

Harvest 9 Grain Rye Bread

Pour water into a 3 to 4 qt glass mixing bowl.

> 14 oz cool tap Water

Add salt, yeast, sugar, seeds, grains, and olive oil... give a quick stir to combine.

> 1-1/2 tsp Salt
> 1/4 tsp Instant Yeast
> 1 Tbsp Sugar
> 2 Tbsp Caraway Seeds
> 1/2 cup King Arthur Harvest Grains Blend
> 1 Tbsp extra-virgin Olive Oil

Add flour... stir until dough forms a shaggy ball, then tumble dough to combine moist flour on the bottom with dry flour, scrape flour from side of bowl and finish combining.

> 2 cups Bread Flour
> 1 cup Rye Flour

Cover bowl with plastic wrap, place in a warm draft-free location, and proof for 8 to 24 hours.

8 to 24 hours later (Dutch oven)

When dough has risen and developed its gluten structure... spray an 8" proofing skillet with no-stick cooking spray and set aside.

Start by putting handle end of spoon in center of dough and "degas, pull and stretch" dough to form a ball.

Generously dust dough and side of bowl with flour... roll dough in flour to coat.

Roll dough out of bowl into proofing skillet.

Place proofing skillet in a warm draft-free location, cover with a lint-free towel, and proof for 1 to 2 hours.

1 to 2 hours later

Before dough is fully proofed... move rack to lower third of oven, place baking vessel in oven, and pre-heat to 450 degrees F.

When oven has come to temperature...

Remove baking vessel from oven, transfer dough from proofing skillet to baking vessel, score (optional) and bake for 30 minutes with the top on and 3 to 15 minutes with the top off depending on how rustic (hard) you like your crust.

30 to 45 minutes later

Gently turn loaf out on work surface and place on cooling rack.

Torpedo Baguettes (baguette pans – 4 loaves)

I use thin baguettes for torpedo sandwiches. And... I used 2 Matfer 311141 double loaf French bread pan (18"x 2") to shape these loaves because it has a smooth baking surface. I used to use a perforated baguette pan, but I had too much trouble with the dough sticking in the perforations.

Torpedo Baguettes

Pour water into a 3 to 4 qt glass mixing bowl.

> 12 oz cool tap Water

Add salt and yeast... give a quick stir to combine.

> 1-1/2 tsp Salt
> 1/4 tsp Instant Yeast

Add flour... stir until dough forms a shaggy ball, then tumble dough to combine moist flour on the bottom with dry flour, scrape flour from side of bowl and finish combining.

> 3 cups Bread Flour

Cover bowl with plastic wrap, place in a warm draft-free location, and proof for 8 to 24 hours.

8 to 24 hours later (baguette pans – 4 loaves)

When dough has risen and developed its gluten structure... spray baguette pan with no-stick cooking spray and set aside.

Start by putting handle end of spoon in center of dough and "degas, pull and stretch" dough to form a ball.

Generously dust dough and side of bowl with flour... roll dough in flour to coat.

Roll dough (and excess flour) out of bowl onto work surface.

Divide dough into 4 portions.

Then (one portion at a time) roll and stretch dough into 16" loafs (dusting with flour as needed), and place in baguette pan. (As you roll the dough on the work surface to shape... it may resist shaping. Try picking the dough up by one end and allow gravity to stretch the dough. Then go back to rolling the dough on the work surface to shape.)

Place pan in a warm draft-free location, cover with a lint-free towel, and proof for 1 to 2 hours.

1 to 2 hours later

Before dough is fully proofed... move rack to middle of oven and pre-heat to 450 degrees F.

When oven has come to temperature...

Bake for 15 minutes.

15 minutes later

Gently turn loaves out on work surface and place on cooling rack.

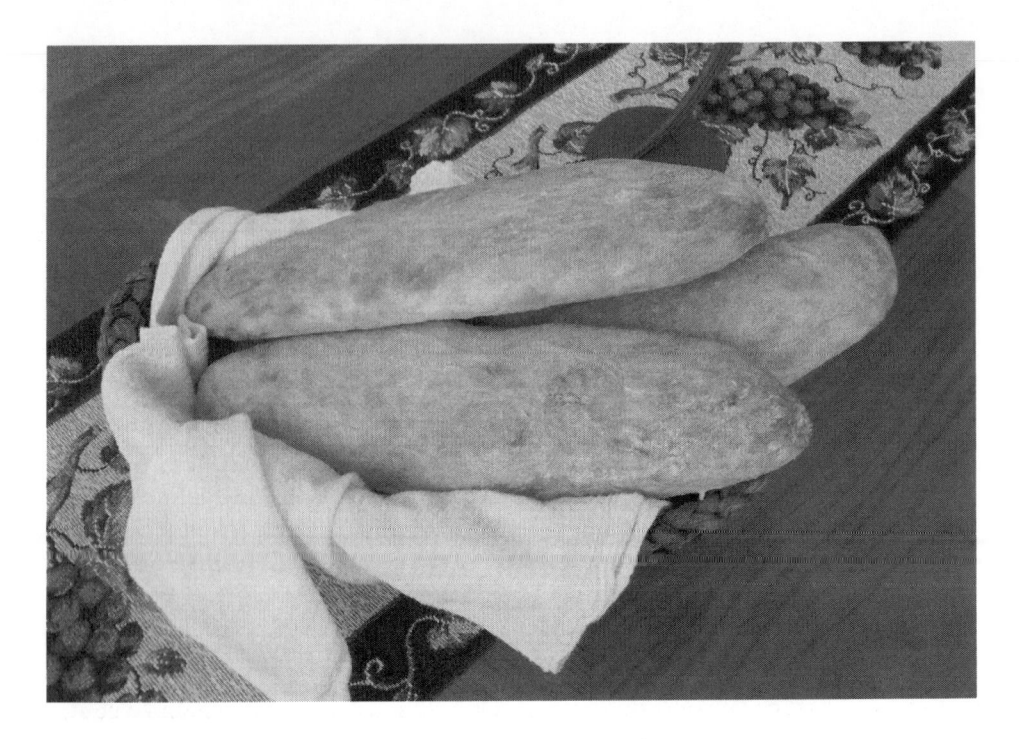

American Baguettes (baguette pans – 3 loaves)

Baguettes are very popular because of their shape. I use these baguettes for sandwiches, cheese bread and bruschetta. And… I used 2 Matfer 311141 double loaf French bread pan (18"x 2") to shape these loaves because it has a smooth baking surface. I used to use a perforated baguette pan, but I had too much trouble with the dough sticking in the perforations.

American Baguettes

Pour water into a 3 to 4 qt glass mixing bowl.

   12 oz cool tap Water

Add salt and yeast... give a quick stir to combine.

   1-1/2 tsp Salt

   1/4 tsp Instant Yeast

Add flour... stir until dough forms a shaggy ball, then tumble dough to combine moist flour on the bottom with dry flour, scrape flour from side of bowl and finish combining.

   3 cups Bread Flour

Cover bowl with plastic wrap, place in a warm draft-free location, and proof for 8 to 24 hours.

8 to 24 hours later (baguette pans – 3 loaves)

When dough has risen and developed its gluten structure... spray baguette pan with no-stick cooking spray and set aside.

Start by putting handle end of spoon in center of dough and "degas, pull and stretch" dough to form a ball.

Generously dust dough and side of bowl with flour... roll dough in flour to coat.

Roll dough (and excess flour) out of bowl onto work surface.

Divide dough into 3 portions.

Then (one portion at a time) roll and stretch dough into 14" loafs (dusting with flour as needed), and place in baguette pan.

Place pans in a warm draft-free location, cover with a lint-free towel, and proof for 1 to 2 hours.

1 to 2 hours later

Before dough is fully proofed... move rack to middle of oven and pre-heat to 450 degrees F.

When oven has come to temperature...

Bake for 20 minutes.

20 minutes later

Gently turn loaves out on work surface and place on cooling rack.

Ciabatta (parchment paper - half loaves)
Ciabatta is very popular for sandwich rolls, cheese bread and crostini. These rolls were baked in the open oven on parchment paper.

Ciabatta

Pour water into a 3 to 4 qt glass mixing bowl.

> 12 oz cool tap Water

Add salt and yeast... give a quick stir to combine.

> 1-1/2 tsp Salt
>
> 1/4 tsp Instant Yeast

Add flour... stir until dough forms a shaggy ball, then tumble dough to combine moist flour on the bottom with dry flour, scrape flour from side of bowl and finish combining.

> 3 cups Bread Flour

Cover bowl with plastic wrap, place in a warm draft-free location, and proof for 8 to 24 hours.

8 to 24 hours later (parchment paper – half loaves)

When dough has risen and developed its gluten structure... place a sheet of parchment paper on a cookie sheet and set aside.

Start by putting handle end of spoon in center of dough and "degas, pull and stretch" dough to form a ball.

Generously dust dough and side of bowl with flour... roll dough in flour to coat.

Roll dough (and excess flour) out of bowl onto work surface.

Divide dough into 2 portions.

Then (one portion at a time) roll dough on work surface (dusting with flour as needed), form a long loaf, and place on parchment paper.

Place in a warm draft-free location, cover with a lint-free towel, and proof for 1 to 2 hours.

1 to 2 hours later

Before dough is fully proofed... move rack to the middle of oven and pre-heat to 450 degrees F.

When oven has come to temperature...

Bake for 25 minutes.

25 minutes later

Gently turn loaves out on work surface and place on cooling rack.

Rosemary Demi Loaves (parchment paper – demi loaves)

I was so thrilled with the appetizer loaves at *Macaroni Grill* that I decided to make my own and developed a rosemary demi loaf recipe that required kneading. Then my wife found a no-knead ciabatta bread recipe in the local newspaper... I was converted. I experimented with no-knead recipes and converted my old rosemary demi loaf recipe to the no-knead method. That was the beginning and I haven't looked back.

I like to give each guest their own loaf so they can use their hands to tear off a piece and dip it in olive oil. Before serving I like to give my guests a choice of straight olive oil, or with a splash of balsamic vinegar, or fresh ground black pepper, or my favorite... a dash or two of Montreal Steak Seasoning added to the olive oil. And we love to serve them with our Smart & Easy Spaghetti and Meatballs. I baked these rolls on our baking stone.

Rosemary Demi Loaves

Pour water into a 3 to 4 qt glass mixing bowl.

13 oz cool tap Water

Add salt, yeast, sugar, rosemary and olive oil... give a quick stir to combine.

1-1/2 tsp Salt

1/4 tsp Instant Yeast

1 Tbsp Sugar

1 Tbsp dried Rosemary

1 Tbsp extra-virgin Olive Oil

Add flour... stir until dough forms a shaggy ball, then tumble dough to combine moist flour on the bottom with dry flour, scrape flour from side of bowl and finish combining.

3 cups Bread Flour

Cover bowl with plastic wrap, place in a warm draft-free location, and proof for 8 to 24 hours.

8 to 24 hours later (parchment paper - demi loaves)

When dough has risen and developed its gluten structure... place a sheet of parchment paper on a cookie sheet and set aside.

Start by putting handle end of spoon in center of dough and "degas, pull and stretch" dough to form a ball.

Generously dust dough and side of bowl with flour... roll dough in flour to coat.

Roll dough (and excess flour) out of bowl onto work surface.

Divide dough into 6 portions.

Then (one portion at a time) roll dough in flour on work surface (dusting with flour as needed) to form a ball, shape rolls by using your fingers to stretch the top and tuck the dough into the back... and arrange rolls on parchment paper.

Place in a warm draft-free location, cover with a lint-free towel, and proof for 1 to 2 hours.

1 to 2 hours later

Before dough is fully proofed... move rack to lower third of oven, insert baking stone, and pre-heat to 450 degrees F.

When oven has come to temperature...

Baste rolls with olive oil, garnish with kosher salt and rosemary, and score.

Extra-virgin Olive Oil

Kosher Salt

Rosemary

When the rolls are ready... slide the parchment paper off the cookie sheet onto the baking stone and bake for 20 minutes.

20 minutes later

Gently turn demi loaves out on work surface and place on cooling rack.

Jalapeño Cheese Bread (long covered baker – half loaves)

If you like jalapeños you will love this bread. This is a nice medium hot jalapeño cheese bread that will blow your socks off. You won't be able to find anything that compares to it on the shelf and it is remarkably easy to make. I used our *Sassafras* superstone long covered baker to bake these loaves.

Notes: Jalapeño is a very special and unique bread, and I understand there's a wide range of taste when it comes to using heat in food. I used 4 jalapeño peppers in the video, but you can use up to 8 to suit your own personal taste. I used canned whole jalapeño peppers because they're consistent and convenient. I slice them in half, remove the seed and dice.

Pour water into a 3 to 4 qt glass mixing bowl.

> 12 oz cool tap Water

Add salt, yeast, peppers, and oil… give a quick stir to combine.

> 1-1/2 tsp Salt
> 1/4 tsp Instant Yeast
> 4 to 8 seeded and diced Jalapeño Peppers
> 1 Tbsp extra-virgin Olive Oil

Add flour… then cheese (if cheese is added before flour it will be harder to combine the ingredients)… stir until dough forms a shaggy ball, then tumble dough to combine moist flour on the bottom with dry flour, scrape flour from side of bowl and finish combining.

> 3 cups Bread Flour
> 1 cup coarse shredded Cheddar Cheese

Cover bowl with plastic wrap, place in a warm draft-free location, and proof for 8 to 24 hours.

8 to 24 hours later (long covered baker - half loaves)

When dough has risen and developed its gluten structure… set two 10" x 12" sheets of parchment paper off to the set aside.

Start by putting handle end of spoon in center of dough and "degas, pull and stretch" dough to form a ball.

Generously dust dough and side of bowl with flour... roll dough in flour to coat.

Roll dough (and excess flour) out of bowl onto work surface.

Divide dough into 2 portions.

Then (one portion at a time) roll dough on work surface (dusting with flour as needed), form a long loaf, and place on parchment paper.

Place dough in a warm draft-free location, cover with a lint-free towel, and proof for 1 to 2 hours.

1 to 2 hours later

Before dough is fully proofed... move rack to lower third of oven, place baking vessel in oven, and pre-heat to 450 degrees F.

When oven has come to temperature...

Garnish... slice 1 jalapeño pepper in half lengthwise, remove seeds, slice each half in half lengthwise and use 2 strips to garnish each loaf, then top with cheddar cheese.

> 1 seeded and sliced Jalapeño Pepper
> 2 Tbsp coarse shredded Cheddar Cheese

Remove baking vessel from oven, use the parchment paper as a sling to lift dough up, place in baking vessel and bake for 25 minutes with the top on and 5 minutes with the top off.

30 to 45 minutes later

Gently turn loaf out on work surface and place on cooling rack. Repeat process for second half loaf.

Queso Dip in a Jalapeño Cheese Bread Bowl (Dutch oven)

Dress up your appetizer table with a homemade jalapeños cheese bread bowl for your Queso dip. Use the no-knead jalapeños cheese bread recipe to make a boule, hollow out the center, fill with Queso dip and serve. I used a 5 qt Dutch oven to bake this loaf... I wanted a wider loaf for the bowl.

Jalapeño Cheese Bread (for queso dip bowl)

Pour water into a 3 to 4 qt glass mixing bowl.

> 12 oz cool tap Water

Add salt, yeast, peppers, and oil... give a quick stir to combine.

> 1-1/2 tsp Salt
> 1/4 tsp Instant Yeast
> 4 to 8 seeded and diced Jalapeño Peppers
> 1 Tbsp extra-virgin Olive Oil

Add flour... then cheese (if cheese is added before flour it will be harder to combine the ingredients)... stir until dough forms a shaggy ball, then tumble dough to combine moist flour on the bottom with dry flour, scrape flour from side of bowl and finish combining.

> 3 cups Bread Flour
> 1 cup coarse shredded Cheddar Cheese

Cover bowl with plastic wrap, place in a warm draft-free location, and proof for 8 to 24 hours.

8 to 24 hours later (Dutch oven)

When dough has risen and developed its gluten structure... spray an 8" proofing skillet with no-stick cooking spray.

Garnish... sprinkle proofing skillet with cheddar cheese, then slice 2 jalapeño pepper in half lengthwise, remove seeds, slice each strip in half and place around the edge of the skillet.

> 2 Tbsp coarse shredded Cheddar Cheese
> 2 seeded and diced Jalapeño Peppers

Start by putting handle end of spoon in center of dough and "degas, pull and stretch" dough to form a ball.

Roll dough out of bowl into proofing skillet.

Place proofing skillet in a warm draft-free location, cover with a lint-free towel, and proof for 1 to 2 hours.

1 to 2 hours later

Before dough is fully proofed... move rack to lower third of oven, place baking vessel in oven, and pre-heat to 450 degrees F.

When oven has come to temperature...

Remove baking vessel from oven, transfer dough from proofing skillet to baking vessel (invert so that garnished and basted bottom is on top), score (optional) and bake for 30 minutes with the top on and 3 to 5 minutes with the top off depending on how rustic (hard) you like your crust.

30 to 35 minutes later

Gently turn loaf out on work surface and place on cooling rack.

Ro*Tel Famous Queso Dip

Pour undrained tomatoes and chilies into 10" non-stick skillet.

> 1 can (10 oz) Ro*Tel Diced Tomatoes & Green Chilies

Dice Velveeta into 1/2-inch cubes and add to tomatoes.

> 1 pkg (16 oz) Velveeta

Add chili.

> 1 can Hormel Chili (optional)

Turn cooktop to medium (275 degrees F) until heated then reduce to simmer (175 degrees F). Stir frequently and heat until cheese is completely melted and mixture is well blended (remember, you don't need to cook cheese... it only needs to be melted).

Use a knife to cut an opening in the top of the loaf, remove the crust, and hollow out the center. Then ladle dip into bread bowl and serve warm with bread bits, tortilla chips, crackers or fresh vegetables.

Notes: You can use this recipe to make your own or you can use any store-bought Queso dip... it's the bread bowl that will dress up the appetizer table and make the dip special.

Mediterranean Olive Bread (long covered baker – half loaves)

If a restaurant served you this loaf as their signature bread... you'd be talking about it for years and you'd be surprised how easy it is to make. I used our *Sassafras* superstone oblong covered baker to shape these loaves.

Mediterranean Olive Bread

Prepare flavor ingredients… zest lemon, slice green olives in half, slice kalamata olives in thirds, and set aside.

> Zest of 1 Lemon
> 2-1/4 oz (1 can) sliced Black Olives
> 1 can stuffed Green Olives (use black olive can to measure)
> 1 can pitted Kalamata Olives (use black olive can to measure)

Pour water into a 3 to 4 qt glass mixing bowl.

> 12 oz cool tap Water

Add salt, yeast, thyme, and olive oil… give a quick stir to combine.

> 1-1/2 tsp Salt
> 1/4 tsp Instant Yeast
> 1 tsp dried Thyme
> 1 Tbsp extra-virgin Olive Oil

Add flour… then flavor ingredients. Stir until dough forms a shaggy ball, tumble to absorb remaining flour, scrape flour from side of bowl and finish combining.

> 3 cups Bread Flour

Cover bowl with plastic wrap, place in a warm draft-free location, and proof for 8 to 24 hours.

8 to 24 hours later (long covered baker - half loaves)

When dough has risen and developed its gluten structure… set two 10" x 12" sheets of parchment paper off to the set aside.

Start by putting handle end of spoon in center of dough and "degas, pull and stretch" dough to form a ball.

Generously dust dough and side of bowl with flour… roll dough in flour to coat.

Roll dough (and excess flour) out of bowl onto work surface.

Divide dough into 2 portions.

Then (one portion at a time) roll dough on work surface (dusting with flour as needed), form a long loaf, and place on parchment paper.

Place dough in a warm draft-free location, cover with a lint-free towel, and proof for 1 to 2 hours.

1 to 2 hours later

Before dough is fully proofed… move rack to lower third of oven, place baking vessel in oven, and pre-heat to 450 degrees F.

When oven has come to temperature…

Remove baking vessel from oven, use the parchment paper to lift the dough up and place it in the baking vessel, score (optional) and bake for 25 minutes with the top on and 5 minutes with the top off.

30 to 45 minutes later

Gently turn loaf out on work surface and place on cooling rack. Repeat process for second half loaf.

Mediterranean Focaccia (rimmed baking sheet)

Focaccia is a flatbread with a long and rich tradition and as flexible as pizza... you can use a wide range of seasonings and flavor ingredients. This focaccia has a beautiful airy crumb and olive oil flavored curst. I baked the focaccia in a standard quarter sheet (9"x12" rimmed baking sheet).

Mediterranean Focaccia

Pour water into a 3 to 4 qt glass mixing bowl.

> 12 oz cool tap Water

Add salt and yeast... give a quick stir to combine.

> 1-1/2 tsp Salt
> 1/4 tsp Instant Yeast
> 2 Tbsp extra-virgin Olive Oil

Add flour... stir until dough forms a shaggy ball, then tumble dough to combine moist flour on the bottom with dry flour, scrape flour from side of bowl and finish combining.

> 3 cups Bread Flour — 120g × 3

Cover bowl with plastic wrap, place in a warm draft-free location, and proof for 8 to 24 hours.

8 to 24 hours later (rimmed baking sheet)

When dough has risen and developed its gluten structure... move rack to lower third of oven and pre-heat to 450 degrees F. Then generously drizzle a 9"x12" rimmed baking sheet with olive oil, spread to coat, and set aside.

Start by putting handle end of spoon in center of dough and "degas, pull and stretch" dough to form a ball.

Generously dust dough and side of bowl with flour... roll dough in flour to coat.

Roll dough out of bowl directly into rimmed baking sheet.

Press to flatten until dough completely covers baking sheet. Then use the tips of your fingers to make dimple in the dough (the dimples are intended to hold olive oil), and season to taste.

> Extra-virgin Olive Oil
> Garlic Salt
> Italian Herb Seasoning
> Rosemary, basil, etc. (optional)

Add olives

> 1-1/4 oz (1/2 can) sliced Black Olives
> 12 stuffed Green Olives (cut in half width-wise)
> 8 Kalamata olives (cut length-wise)
> Tomatoes, etc. (optional)

Because flatbreads are typically bake without a 2nd proofing... it's ready for the oven.

When oven has come to temperature...

Bake for 25 minutes.

25 minutes later

Serve as you would a pizza.

Printed in Great Britain
by Amazon.co.uk, Ltd.,
Marston Gate.